ANIMAL COLORING BOOK

This Book Belongs To

COLOR TEST PAGE

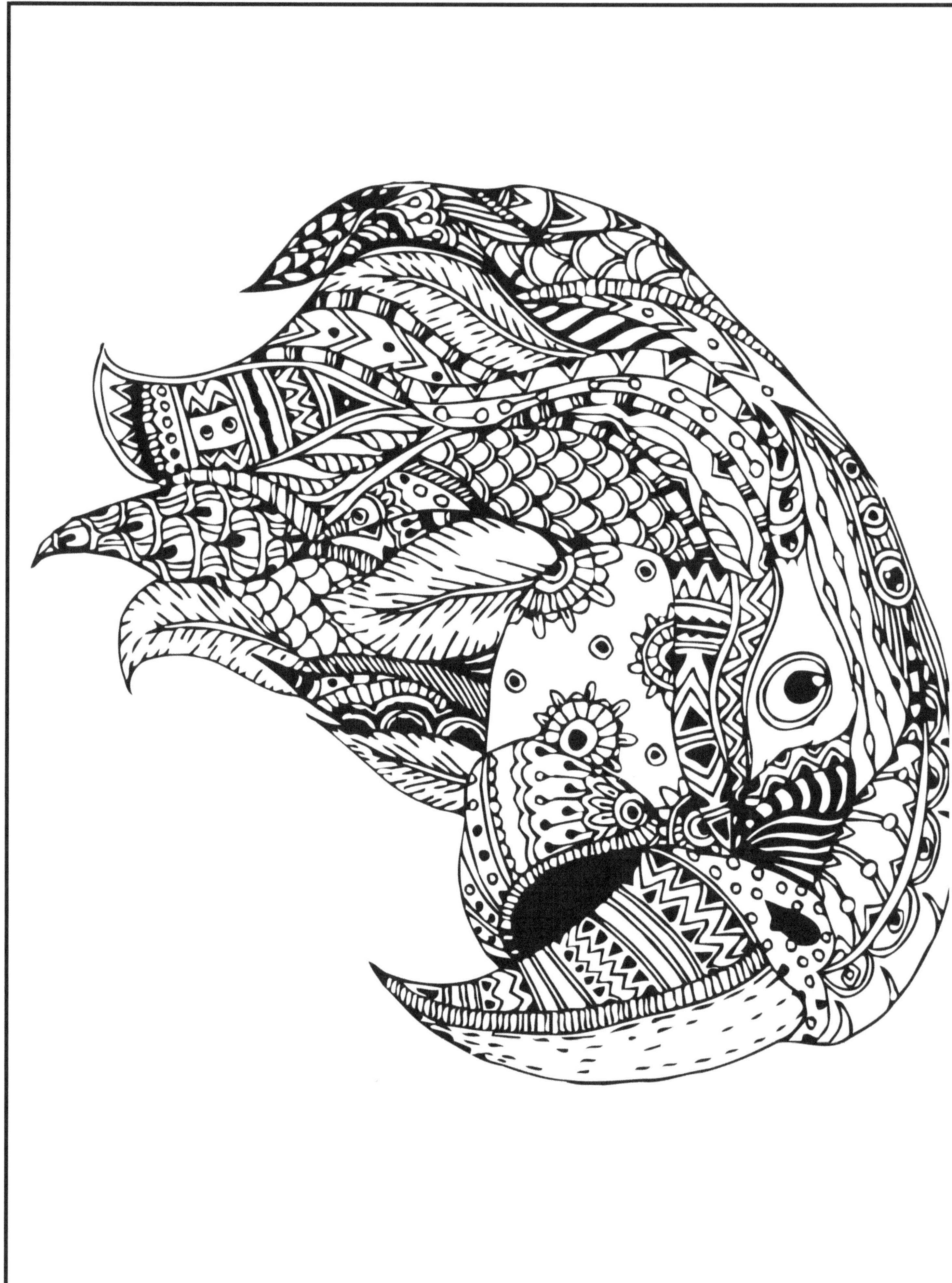

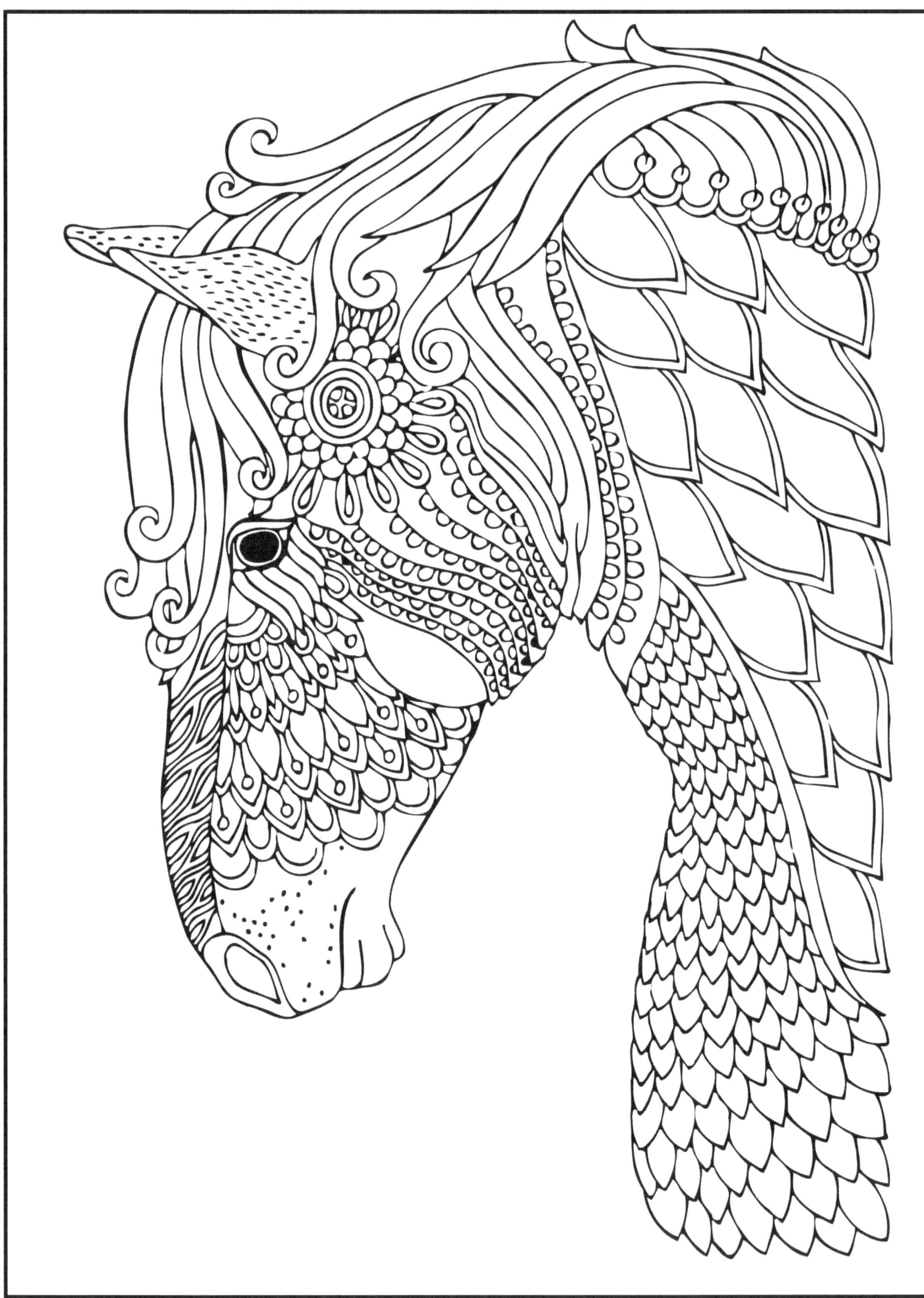

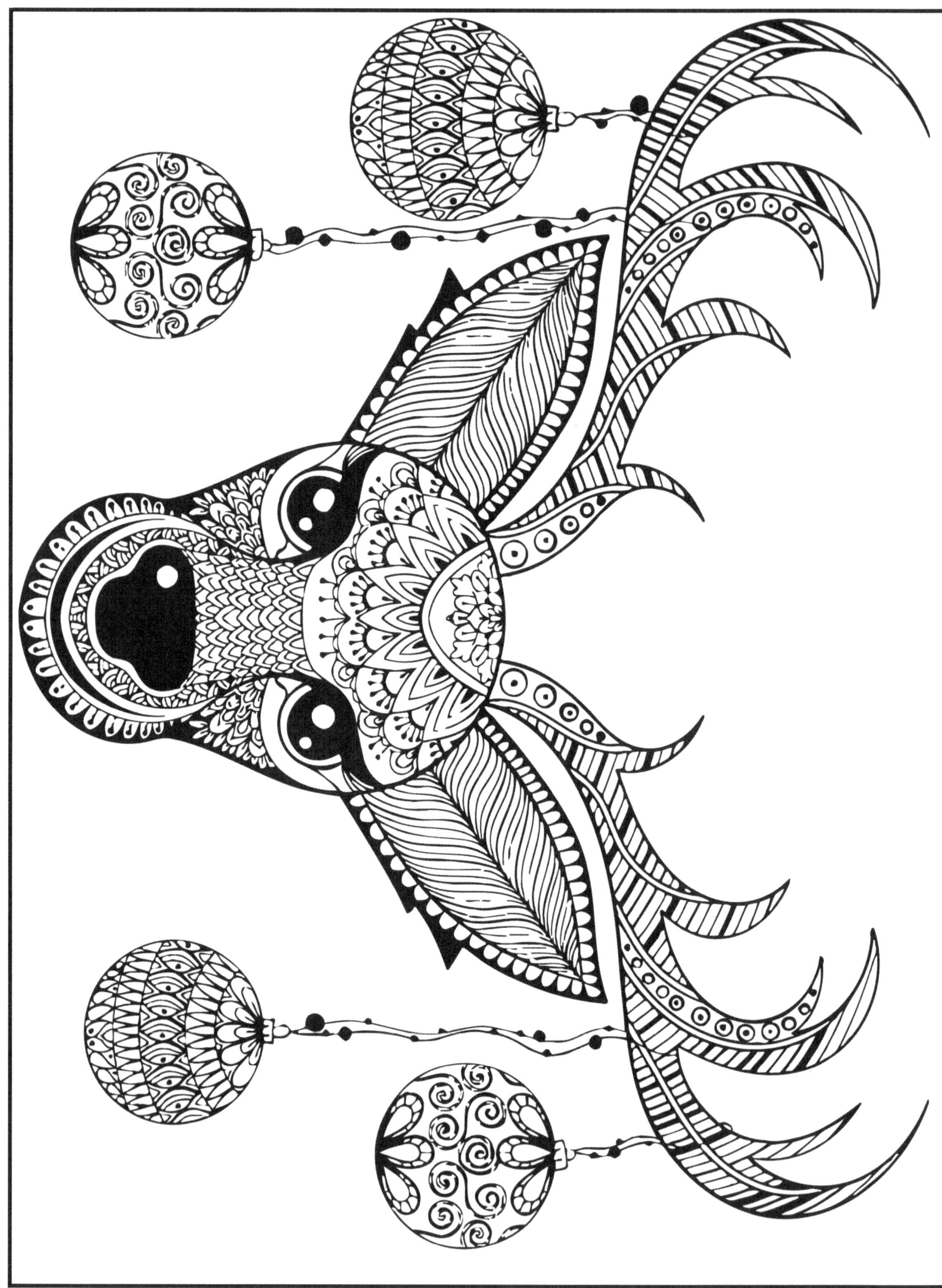

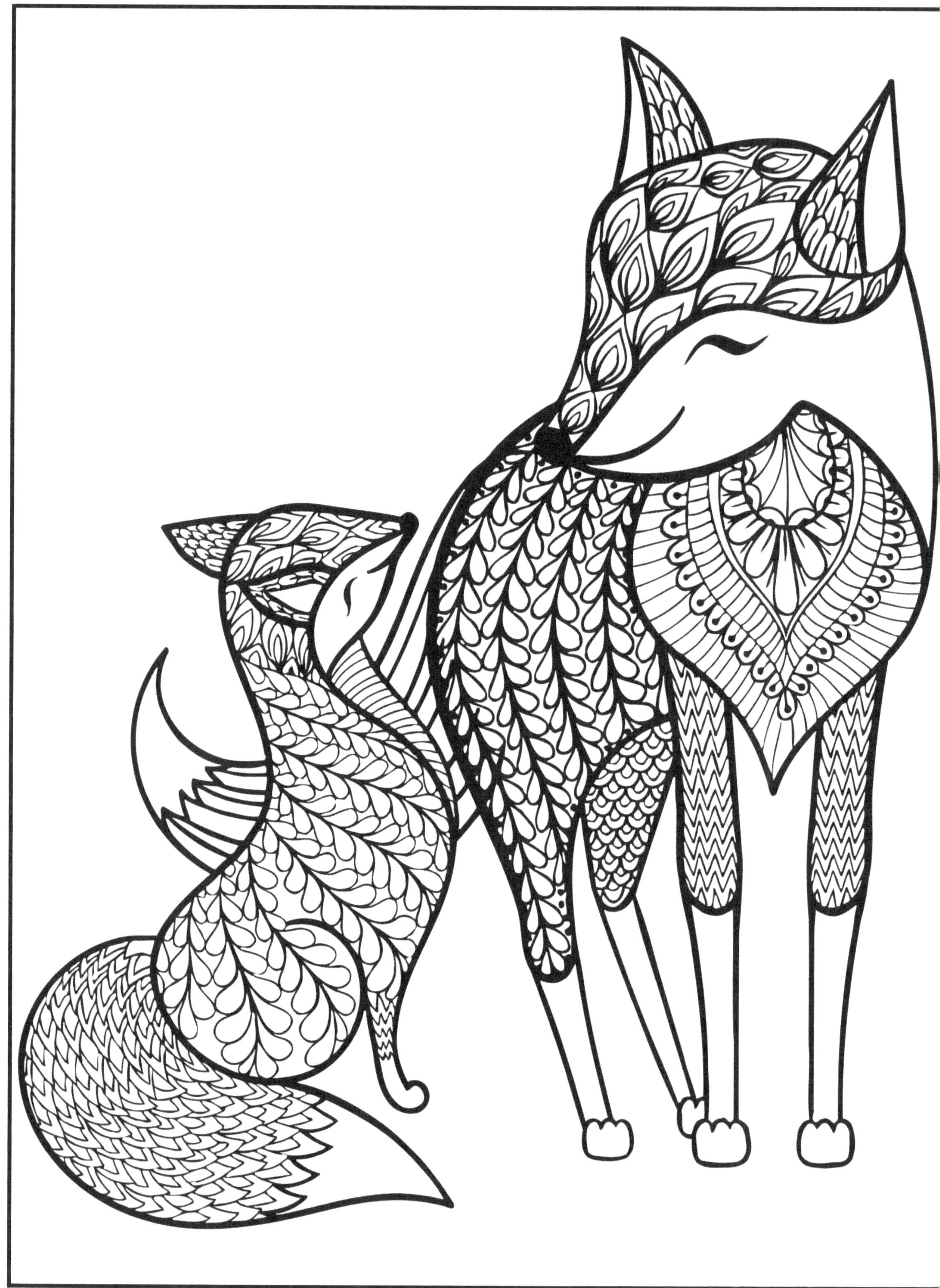

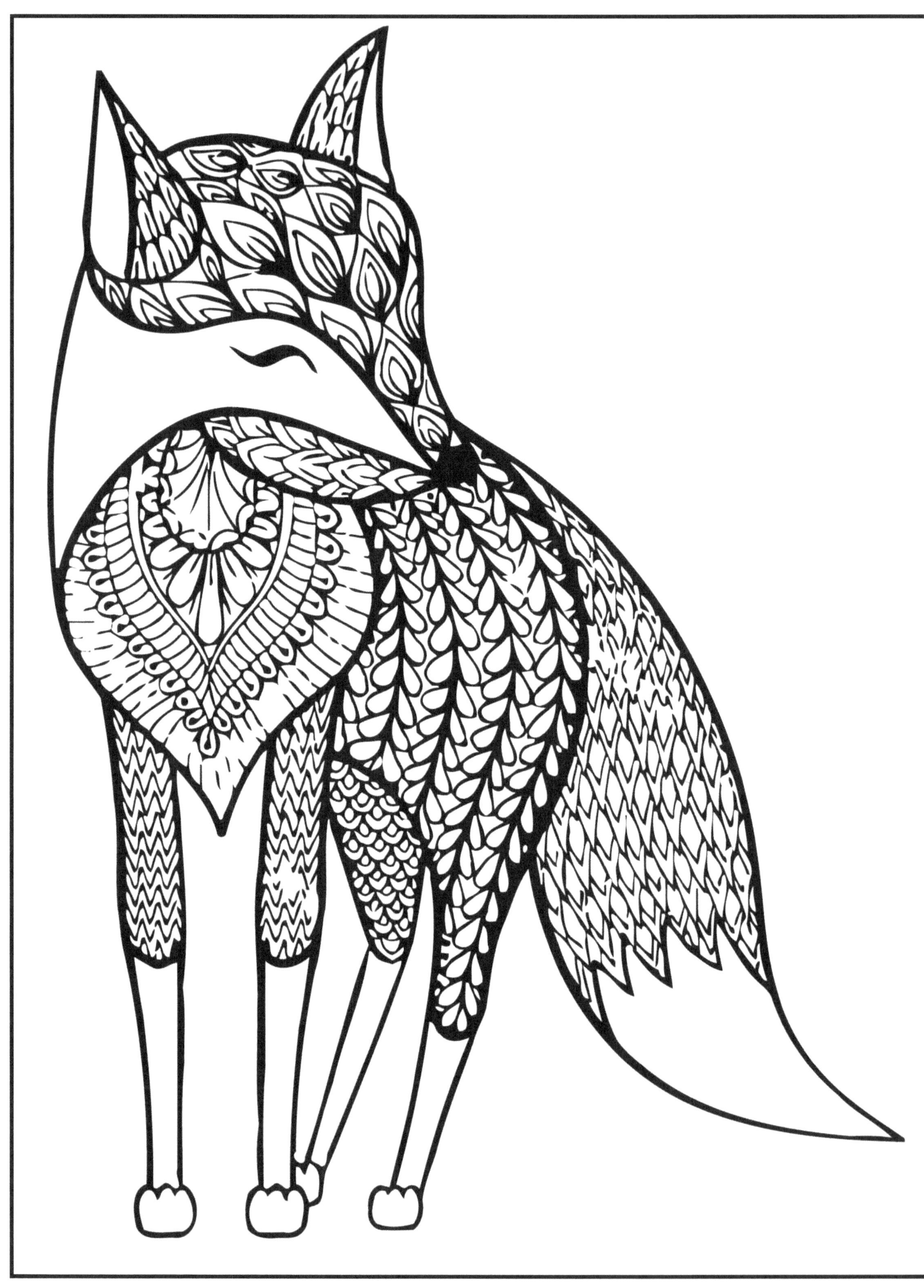

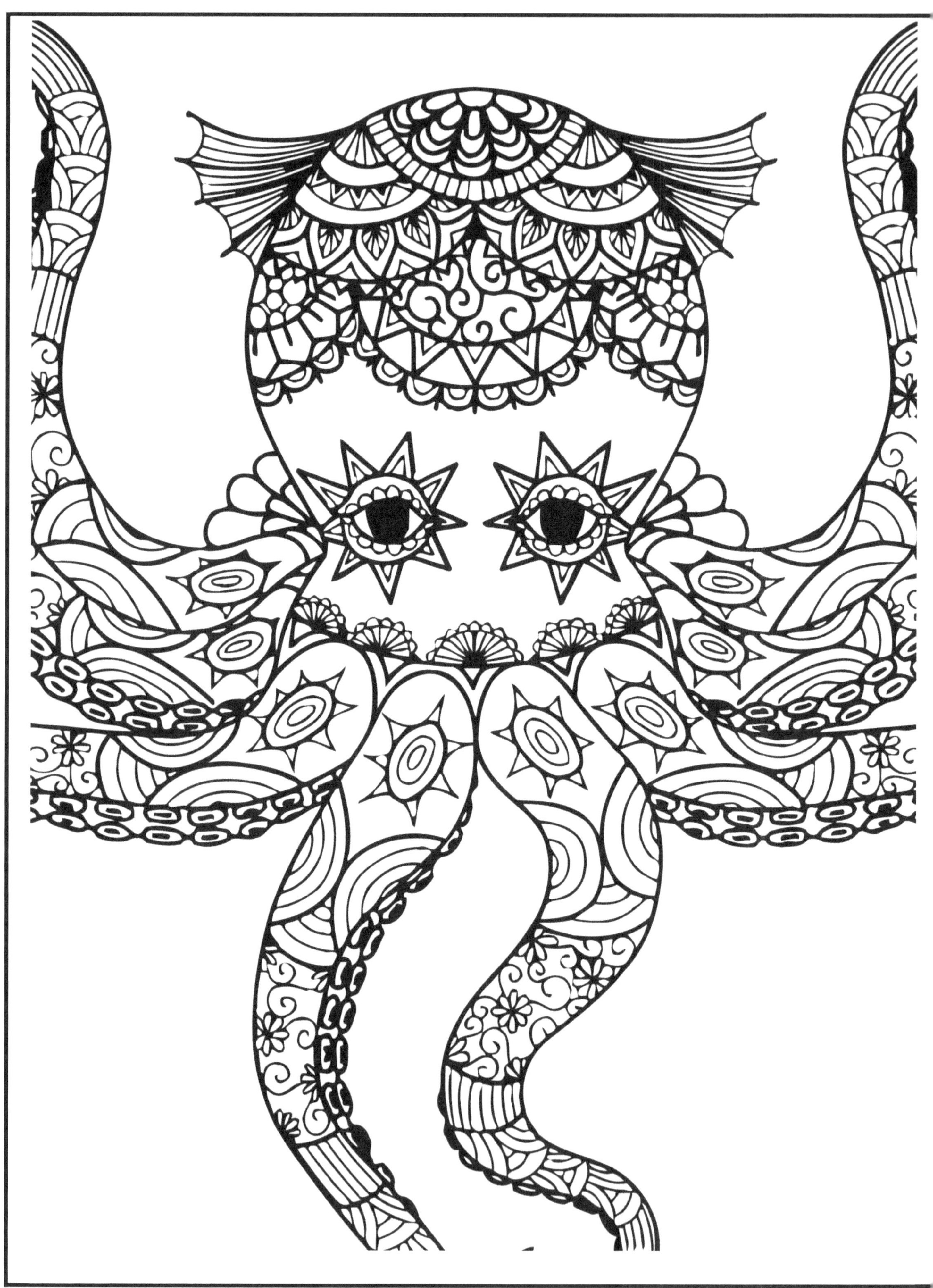